PENGUIN BOOKS

A BOY AT THE HOGARTH PRESS

Richard Kennedy was educated at Marlborough. At sixteen, having failed to achieve an adequate academic standard, he left and went to work at the Hogarth Press.

After he left the Hogarth Press he took a journalists' course at University College, London, and subsequently he went to the Regent Street Polytechnic where he worked industriously as an art student for two years. In the years preceding the war he worked in an advertising agency. He married Olive Johnstone whom he had met at University College and has three children.

During the war Richard Kennedy served in the RAF ground staff and rose to the rank of Corporal. Since then he has occupied himself in illustrating children's books, which are known to children throughout the world. He has also written *A Parcel of Time*, a record of his life before he joined the Hogarth Press.

RICHARD KENNEDY

A Boy
at the
Hogarth
Press

ILLUSTRATED BY THE AUTHOR

with an Introduction by Bevis Hillier

PENGUIN BOOKS

Penguin Books Ltd, Harmondsworth, Middlesex, England
Penguin Books, 625 Madison Avenue, New York, New York 10022, U.S.A.
Penguin Books Australia Ltd, Ringwood, Victoria, Australia
Penguin Books Canada Ltd, 2801 John Street, Markham, Ontario, Canada L3R 1B4
Penguin Books (N.Z.) Ltd, 182–190 Wairau Road, Auckland 10, New Zealand

—

First published in a limited edition by The Whittington Press 1972
Published by Heinemann Educational Books Ltd 1972
Published in Penguin Books 1978

—

—

Made and printed in Great Britain by
Richard Clay (The Chaucer Press) Ltd,
Bungay, Suffolk
Set in Monotype Caslon

TO OLIVE

PUBLISHERS' NOTE

The publishers wish to point out that these reminiscences, cast in the form of a diary, were written some forty years after the events they describe.

ACKNOWLEDGEMENTS are due to Quentin Bell and Angelica Garnett for permission to quote the passage on page 17 from *To the Lighthouse*, published by the Hogarth Press.

INTRODUCTION

THIS book can be thought of, in no way unkindly, as a
sort of literary *Diary of a Nobody*. Richard Kennedy went
to work for Leonard and Virginia Woolf at the Hogarth
Press in 1928 when he was sixteen. His status was practically that of a fly on the wall; Francis Birrell (who had
also worked at the Hogarth Press) asked him at a Bloomsbury party whether he was a factotum, adding 'More
totem than fact, I should imagine.' He was of no conse-
quence to the paladins of Bloomsbury. There was no
reason to exercise their wit and charm on him. He saw
them at their most unguarded and least artificial. That is
what makes his account so fascinating.

After the marmoreal postures of Leonard Woolf's autobiography and the rarified recollections of various Bloomsbury courtiers, Kennedy's wide-eyed view reminds one of
the boy in *The Emperor's New Clothes*. The undress man-
ners of the Woolfs were less exquisite than their literary
ones. Leonard Woolf screams with rage, swears, and tells
Kennedy he is 'the most frightful idiot he has ever had
the privilege of meeting in a long career of suffering fools'.
Of Mrs Woolf, Kennedy notes: 'I think she is rather
cruel in spite of the kind, rather dreamy way she looks at
you. She described Mrs Cartwright as having the step of
an elephant and the ferocity of a tiger, which gives a very
false impression as Ma Cartwright has no ferocity at all,
although she does charge about everywhere.' To this
Kennedy adds, in a phrase as characteristic of his nature
as of the time about which he is writing, 'I consider it bad
form to laugh at your employees.'

Kennedy was naïf: few boys of sixteen, short of John Stuart Mill or Aldous Huxley, are not. He confused D. H. Lawrence with TE, eschatology with scatology, and when he asked Virginia Woolf what Proust was like (for a reviewer had called her 'The English Proust') he rhymed the word with Faust: 'At first she did not understand ... but she laughed and said she couldn't do French cooking, but it was very delicious.'

But his naïveté is his greatest asset. He has the raw adolescent honesty which Denton Welch died with and which Rousseau never grew out of. Rawness is also sensitivity: with no social carapace, no excessive surface wit to deflect or mangle the truth, he was then what Wyndham Lewis called 'the revolutionary simpleton': one who asks questions which the sophisticated are afraid to ask, and who therefore gets answers they never find. The book with which this has most in common is George Moore's *Confessions of a Young Man*.

One of the delights of the book is the line drawings by Kennedy, drawn from memory. On first seeing them, I thought the dominant influence must be Augustus John, but then I read Kennedy's narrative and found that he had been impressed at that most impressionable age by the work of Gaudier-Brzeska: 'I have been practising this type of drawing and am going to the zoo on Saturday to do some.' Kennedy's writing reveals the same economical notation of telling detail. The first meeting with Leonard Woolf; Woolf at the Press; his own adventures with a shelf; a picnic on the Downs; Leonard Woolf as 'the magician who keeps us all going by the strength of his will – like the one in the *Tales of Hoffmann*'; Virginia as 'a beautiful magical doll, very precious, but sometimes uncontrollable. Perhaps, like the doll, she hasn't got a soul.'

A master writer of chronic over-refinement, such as

Max Beerbohm or Lytton Strachey, would have teased all these details into a brilliant fantasia, as seductive and factual as a mirage – as Max did in the account of Swinburne at 'The Pines'. But with Kennedy, we know we are never being bamboozled for the sake of a literary effect. He has his set pieces too, and they are all the funnier because they have gained nothing in the telling: the collapse of the famous shelf on Lord Oliver; selling Dostoyevsky to a Sheffield librarian; a Bloomsbury cricket match; Ivy Compton-Burnett coming to tea after Woolf's unfortunate rejection of *Brothers and Sisters*. If only all art criticism were as plain spoken as his account of the banned exhibition of D. H. Lawrence's paintings. Sometimes his gaucheness is positively inspired – as when he was asked by Mrs Boris Anrep what he thought of Mrs Woolf's books, and replied, with perfect justice, that he didn't think she created characters as well as Turgenev. 'I could see this didn't go down at all well and felt rather like Peter denying Christ.'

In the five volumes of Leonard Woolf's autobiography, there is only one curt sentence about Richard Kennedy. But no biographer of Mrs Woolf will be able to disregard Kennedy's book, and it is arguable that it will tell him more of her true character than Woolf does in his frigid, studied and much expurgated account. Certainly the character of Leonard Woolf is shown here less masked: his temper, his taste for accounts and distaste for lavatory humour.

In November 1966, the *New Statesman* (of which Leonard Woolf was still a Director) invited competitors in its Weekend Competition 'to provide an excerpt from some as yet unpublished Bloomsbury memoir'. Immodestly, and not even very relevantly, I shall quote my winning entry:

As I came into the drawing-room Lytton was teetering about in a pair of Ot's high-heeled shoes, while the *châtelaine* of Garsington herself applied violet salve to her face in front of the looking-glass, jutting out her chin exactly as in the Augustus John portrait. Seeing me, Lytton stopped cavorting and virtually collapsed on to a settle, pale and coughing. After a while he began to write, with that desperate vivacity which suggested he had only another 23 years to live. Virginia, radiantly emaciated, wandered to the window, and stood looking out over Coram's Fields. Lytton's pen sped on with planchette facility. Quite suddenly, I had the curious and rather nightmarish impression that we were all living in the real world. But it was only momentary. Virginia lit a joss-stick, Lytton warbled something about Madame du Deffand's poodle, and Ot began dancing a rigadoon.

It is one of the merits of Richard Kennedy's book that it shows us the Bloomsbury group living indeed in the real world: how Rodmell, so idyllic in the photographs, stank of the cesspool; the ethereal Mrs Woolf rolled her own shag cigarettes; Leonard Woolf concerned himself with the petty cash. But it would be wrong to regard the book as merely a new sidelight on Bloomsbury. It is also a study of an adolescent finding his depth in a super-civilized society. A subject which Henry James or L. P. Hartley, Iris Murdoch or Cyril Connolly could develop with all the nuances discernible in an objective view, but none with such a convincing impression of what a raw teenager, not a subtle novelist, might feel in such circumstances. All of them perhaps understand the rock pool too well and the fish too little. By the end of this narrative, Richard Kennedy is leaving that glittering lagoon, with its strange polyps and vicious cross-currents, and is heading for the open sea.

BEVIS HILLIER

A BOY AT THE
HOGARTH PRESS

'What you need to do is to get behind the counter, Richard.'

My Uncle George was speaking on the beach at Carbis Bay, St Ives.

The counter he was referring to was that of the Hogarth Press, run by Leonard and Virginia Woolf, which at that time, in the late twenties, was becoming the forum of the Bloomsbury Group.

I was sixteen and had just been superannuated from Marlborough after I had failed, during three and a half years, to get beyond Lower School.

An informal discussion was going on about my future, in which my aunt and my mother, though present, took little part – busying themselves with Thermos flasks.

My uncle explained that he had met Leonard Woolf at the Cranium Club and, hearing that he was on the look-out for 'a likely young man', had persuaded him to take me on as an apprentice publisher.

In response to my objection that I was not cut out for a 'brainy' job, my uncle was at some pains to point out that intellectual brilliance was not necessarily as much of an advantage in an apprentice as the ability to make himself useful about the place without getting in the way.

Gazing out to sea, he went on to enlarge on the virtues of a good apprentice – these were personified by the conduct of a boy in my uncle's office named Sternfield. An eminent architect,* Uncle George employed several apprentices, among whom was Lady Pansy Pakenham, who was friendly with Evelyn Waugh, a slim young man always ready to help one on with one's coat. Lady Pansy was very beautiful, but unlike Sternfield, she failed to keep her pencils sharpened or faithfully record telephone messages.

Sternfield never lost a plan, he replenished stocks of drawing materials, and he put up Useful Shelves.

My Uncle George had taken up architecture after starting a promising career as a painter, which was cut short by an eye disorder. By the time his sight had recovered he felt it was too late to carry on with painting and he chose architecture as a more practical way of supporting a large family.

He had a great admiration for business efficiency, although he lacked it himself – which did not prevent him landing a number of lucrative contracts.

It is impossible to travel about London without passing public buildings designed by Uncle George; for instance, the Royal Geographical Society Building and the Chenil Galleries; they are not eye-catching because they blend in so perfectly with their surroundings. He also built a number of charming country houses. The Guinnesses

*George Lawrence Kennedy (1882–1954).

16

were among his clients and they became life-long friends.

After listening to these plans for my future, I mentioned to my uncle my interest in drawing and the possibility that I might become an artist.

My uncle replied that it was a positive duty on the part of any responsible person to discourage a young man or woman from taking up the arts: if they were any good they would do so anyway.

The picnic over, we returned to Talland House – curiously enough, the scene of Virginia Woolf's first successful novel, *To the Lighthouse*. Her parents had rented the house from my aunt's parents. From the windows the lighthouse can be seen far out to sea, separated from land, a symbol of the unattainable.*

A LETTER ARRIVES

Shortly after my mother and I returned from our holiday in St Ives a letter came from Leonard Woolf asking me to call on him.

This was the first letter of this sort that anyone had ever sent to me. I was struck by the orange paper on which it was typed; the symbol of the wolf's head at the top of the letter; its brevity and original layout; and finally the

*'– but here, the houses falling away on both sides, they came out on the quay, and the whole bay spread before them and Mrs Ramsay could not help exclaiming, "Oh, how beautiful!" For the great plateful of blue water was before her; the hoary Lighthouse, distant, austere, in the midst; and on the right, as far as the eye could see, fading and falling, in soft low pleats, the green sand dunes with the wild flowing grasses on them, which always seemed to be running away into some moon country, uninhabited of men.

' "That was the view," she said.'

To the Lighthouse, Penguin edition, p. 16

trembling signature at the bottom which contrived to be firm.

Leonard Woolf did, in fact, look very like a wolf in human form – but an extremely intellectual wolf, not to say a kindly wolf – a very Socrates of wolves.

At this first meeting he sat in the position of Cézanne's gardener with his back to the light from two large windows which looked out on the trees of Tavistock Square. His silhouette presented a number of sharp corners.

The room seemed filled with books and apples and on the floor slept a cocker spaniel.

I was aware of a slight trembling of his head and hands as he bit into a Cox's Orange Pippin. This trembling gave the impression, not of infirmity, but of the vibration of a powerful intellectual machine.

He did not ask me any questions about my academic attainments, but talked about the Hogarth Press and explained that Angus Davidson, a former employee, had failed to press the sales.

'I'll press the sales for you, sir,' I said, thrusting up my hand.

My eagerness seemed to please him. The interview proved to be largely a formality. It was arranged that my salary should be £1 a week for the first six months, during which time it would be seen how I got on, then I was to have a holiday and the position could be reviewed.

He was relieved that I had a portable typewriter of my own and said he would be grateful if I could bring it to the office when I came the following week.

I bounded down the stairs after he showed me out of his flat. I was elated that I had got the job. My sense of failure at school had been all the more intense because I

was not clear in my mind how it had come about. I had
certainly tried hard enough. Nor did I agree with the
school's estimation of my mental equipment. Now I was
getting a second chance to prove myself.

I arrived much too early this morning and had a long wait before Mrs Cartwright and Miss Belcher arrived to open the Press. They both wore overalls: Miss Belcher a flowered one and Ma Cartwright a plain beige one which has a long way to go round her as she is very stout. She has a shock of white hair, pink cheeks and pebble-type glasses through which she blinks nervously. She nearly fell down the area steps when she arrived – she runs everywhere on very high heels and appears to be very efficient, typing at a terrific speed.

Leonard Woolf obviously does not think her at all efficient. In fact he was bloody awful to her in front of Miss Belcher and myself because she tried to cover up some trivial mistake. When he's annoyed, his voice goes up into a sort of exasperated wail, especially when he's saying words like 'Why? ? ?' and 'Absurd! ! !' which he drags out to show how unreasonable something is. He does have a special way of talking which I think comes of the care he takes to say exactly what he means. It's a kind of drawl.

Miss Belcher is quite pretty – I don't know what Todd would think of her. She has a mole on her cheek. We went to lunch together and we had apple turnover.

LW was very nice to me; he asked me to walk round the Square with him. Pinker, LW's spaniel, seems to be

suffering from worms and drags his bottom along the
carpet in the office, but this does not seem to worry LW.

He showed me the printing room and the books.

In the afternoon Mrs W came into the office. She was
very beautifully dressed and called me Mr Kennedy.

MY FIRST DAY – A SMART LITERARY
GATHERING

Mrs W said she was sure I had done enough work for the day and would I like to go to a lecture on Ibsen which was being given by Desmond MacCarthy to help start his magazine, *Life and Letters*. She said I could have her invitation as she had to go to a party.

Desmond MacCarthy talked about Ibsen as a story-teller. I must go to some of Ibsen's plays, especially this one, *Ghosts*. The lecture was in Berkeley Square – masses of Bentleys and flowers. We sat on gold inlaid chairs. After the lecture I bought one of the copies of *Life and Letters*; it had a story by Desmond MacCarthy in it. He seemed rather put out that Mrs W had given me her ticket – I suppose he was counting on her coming.

There is a space in the office where I might put up a shelf.

MY SECOND DAY – HOPES AND FEARS

It's been an unlucky day. I've made a bad start. This morning LW gave me a letter to type returning a rejected MS to an author. I must say the letter was short and none too sweet. LW thinks people can either write or they can't and if they can't it's not worthwhile wasting time over them. The letter was just two lines: 'Dear Sir, We regret we are unable to accept the enclosed MS. Yours faithfully,'. It took me about an hour to type it out under Miss Belcher's scornful eye. I put it into LW's tray and when he came down after lunch he glanced at it and then handed it back to me, pointing with a trembling finger at

the word 'except' which I had written instead of 'accept'.

Perhaps I ought to go to Pitman and take a course in typing. I am feeling very despondent and there are so many things in this job that I will have to do which I am very bad at and never likely to get better at.

For one thing, there are the bagmen who come round from the various booksellers to buy books for cash. Miss Belcher and I are supposed to take it in turn to serve them. This involves working out the discount they receive on the net price of the book; 25 per cent off for less than six copies and 33 per cent for orders over six. I have to work it out laboriously on paper which takes some time. Some of the bagmen are very nice, like Mr Bumpus – an elderly bearded man who waits patiently while I do my calculations.

Gordon & Gotch Export and Simpkin Marshall were in a hurry and had no scruples about ragging me with a wink at Miss Belcher.

The only thing which gives me confidence is the printing. I can do this all right – the machining that is. L W demonstrated the treadle printing machine to me. In spite of his trembling hands he seems to be able to feed the paper in at a high speed. If the paper slips and you make a grab at it, you may lose a hand between the jaws of the machine. It's quite exciting work and I was able to work up quite a high speed after he left. We are printing some poems by Nancy Cunard. L W showed me how to watch the impression and he very delicately adjusted a full stop which had come adrift in its bed of type and was making a dent in the paper.

Looking at the different sized rules and various decorative motifs, I felt I could make some designs for showcards.

The type is locked into metal frames with pieces of

wood called furniture. I made some experiments and printed my name and address to send to Todd.

LW seems to sell a lot of his books by sending out leaflets advertising them. We are never to send out a parcel of books without putting in a range of leaflets. A good idea would be to put up a shelf over the packing bench on which to stack the piles of leaflets, so that Miss Belcher and I don't have to interrupt our slashing-away with knives and string to fetch leaflets. All we would have to do would be to reach up and take the leaflets down from the shelf.

I did not have lunch with Miss Belcher today because LW sent down instructions that we were to lunch separately. This is rather a snub for her, but I think she blamed me for it, not LW, for although she can stand up to him, which Ma Cartwright can't, in her eyes he can do no wrong.

BUSINESS TRAINING

I have started to go to Pitmans. There is a separate entrance for men and women. I find myself drawing the backs of people's heads instead of getting on with my typing.

I am on rather bad terms with my uncle and aunt as I stole their car in order to take a girl out. She is quite a lot older than I am and works in a café by South Kensington Station. I had to pretend to telephone Uncle and Aunt from the garage before the man in charge would let me take the car.

Unfortunately, I hit a bus on the Old Kent Road and damaged the back axle. However, the car limped to Redhill where Yvonne's parents have a farm. I had felt under

31

a moral obligation to carry on as I had given Yvonne my word and she had told her parents all about it.

I told Miss Belcher all about the incident. 'You are getting quite a lad,' she said. I thought of suggesting we should have lunch together in spite of L W, but she picked up her bag and stomped out of the room on her high heels without giving me much encouragement.

A SOCIAL EVENING WITH THE WOOLFS

I went to supper with the Woolfs. We had strawberries and cream. Mrs W was in a very happy mood. She said she had been to a nightclub the night before and how marvellous it was inventing new foxtrot steps. I thought L W's back looked a bit disapproving as he was dishing out the strawberries. The other guest was George Rylands,* a very good-looking young man who had worked for the Woolfs before going to university. We were publishing a book by him called *Words and Poetry* and McKnight Kauffer had done a design for the cover. George Rylands egged Mrs W on to talk about how much she enjoyed kicking up her heels. I couldn't help feeling a little shocked.

Some people came in with huge bundles of flowers to give her. They had been commissioned to write an article about dirt-track racing. As they were very hard up, they were very anxious to get the job, but the editor had turned down their manuscripts. Mrs W had come to their rescue and written a description of the sport, in which she had compared the roaring machines and the arc lights to a medieval tournament.

*George 'Dadie' Rylands (b. 1902). Sometime Bursar, Lecturer and Director of Studies at King's College, Cambridge. The Hogarth Press published his *Words and Poetry* and *Poems*.

Some more people came in after supper. Mrs Woolf started rolling her shag cigarettes. She gave one to an American lady who nearly choked to death.

She started talking about the Hogarth Press in a way that I thought didn't please LW very much, saying it was like keeping a grocer's shop. I think she is rather cruel in spite of the kind rather dreamy way she looks at you. She described Mrs Cartwright as having the step of an elephant and the ferocity of a tiger, which gives a very false impression as Ma Cartwright has no ferocity at all, although she does charge about everywhere. She also described her sliding down the area steps on her bottom, during the frost.

I consider it bad form to laugh at your employees.

June 30, 1928. A LITERARY SWAIN.
MRS W AT WORK

Desmond MacCarthy came into the Press and asked to see Mrs W. But she had given strict instructions she was not to be disturbed so he had to content himself with writing her a note. He took about half an hour to do this, leaning on the high schoolmaster's desk which we use as a counter. It would take him a long time to write his articles in the *Sunday Times* at this rate.

In the door that leads into our office from the back there is a square window through which Mrs W can look to see if the coast is clear to enter the office.

When we have exhausted the parcels of fifty copies of each book which are kept in the office, Miss Belcher and I have to enter her studio and manhandle and open one of the very large bales of 500 that are stored there. Sitting in her little space by the gas fire, she reminds me of the

Bruce Bairnsfather veterans of the War, surrounded by sandbags. She looks at us over the top of her steel-rimmed spectacles, her grey hair hanging over her forehead and a shag cigarette hanging from her lips. She wears a hatchet-blue overall and sits hunched in a wicker armchair with her pad on her knees and a small typewriter beside her.

August 1. THE SHELF

Today the trumpet blasts. I put up my shelf. It proved to be a much harder job than I thought. In the first place I had to walk like Jesus carrying the Cross practically the whole way to Tavistock Square because the conductor refused to let me on the bus with the wood.

It did not take me long to discover that the damp and rotten walls were not going to give much purchase to the Rawlplugs holding the brackets. Great chunks of plaster kept falling off and filling the room with dust.

Finally, but only just, I got the shelf erected. Then, very nervously, I started to pile the circulars onto it.

I expected it to collapse at any moment, but it took their weight. Finally, at eleven o'clock I left triumphant on my way to Russell Square Tube Station.

L W and Mrs W are going down to Rodmell next week, but he will have a chance to see the shelf before he goes.

A LETTER TO A SCHOOL FRIEND

Dear Todd,

How are you getting on in the Upper Fifth, old lad? By the time you leave I shall be a celebrated chap in the literary world, making pots of money!

The Hogarth Press, where I'm working, is in the heart of

the literary world, with authors coming in all the time. Mrs Woolf, wife of the manager, is a very celebrated author and, in her own way, more important than Galsworthy. LW and Mrs W think nothing of Galsworthy.

The premises are a bit smelly as we work in the basement which was the kitchen quarters in an epoch when light and sanitation were not considered important for servants.

The general office has an enormous dresser in which the ledgers are kept. The kitchen range has been taken out and a gas fire and ring put in its place. The typist, Miss Belcher, makes tea on the ring. She is quite pretty, but not up to your sister.*

There is a dark sort of passage running to the back of the building along the sides of which parcels of books are stacked. Several cell-like rooms, which were probably used for the torture of Victorian skivvies lead off it. One of these is used for printing.

The wc is just a cupboard without light with some holes in the door.

At the end of the passage across a small area is a big room with a skylight. This is called the studio and is where Mrs Woolf works. It is full of the large bales of books, each containing about 500 copies, that come from the printers. Their weight makes them suck up the damp from the stone floor and the room smells of mildew.

But this sort of thing does not matter if you are in the literary world. Ma Cartwright runs the office. She is very short and stout and sends me out to buy Banbury and Eccles cakes at the Express Dairy.

I went there for lunch on the first day with the typist, but Mr Woolf has said we must go to lunch separately.

---

*Ann Todd. Became film actress. Best known probably for *The Seventh Veil* (1946) with James Mason.

The house is going to miss me playing Back for them next year. I try to keep in training by going for a run round Battersea Park odd mornings. I wish I could get some rugger.

Yours sincerely,
Drowse

August 2. THE SHELF

Miss Belcher is rather sniffy about the shelf. However, LW is obviously very pleased and congratulated me on it during our walk round the Square. I took the opportunity, as we were going down the area steps, of asking him if he believed in the immortality of the soul. 'Obviously not!' he retorted. I could not help observing that Pinker looked as if he had a soul. As far as LW was concerned, it would be to members of the animal kingdom alone that he would allow souls.

Smells of Steaks in Passageways. I like this poem considerably. I've got in the habit of wandering round the passages off Fleet Street and Farringdon Road when the office sends me out on a job. I like looking down into the basements and seeing a printer's devil like myself drinking a cup of orange coloured tea. The old men with their red noses and greasy bowler hats look as if they were made of something other than flesh and blood – brown paper and melted down string, I should think.

Today I read *The Dark* by Andreyev in a café under the Holborn Viaduct. I like the Russian books better than any others we publish. I was waiting to collect some blocks of a new design for the wolf's head that McKnight Kauffer has done. L W wants to use them facing each other in a three-inch column in the *Observer* which he has taken for next Sunday. I think they will look too crowded in the space. Victor Gollancz buys huge double column advertisements bordered by massive black rules, and Chatto and Windus are advertising Lytton Strachey's *Elizabeth and Essex* very elegantly, all on its own with plenty of white space around it and their colophon beneath.

If we are going to have a new wolf's head, we ought to make a splash.

August 20. TURGENEV

L W and I discussed Turgenev and I have got *Torrents of Spring* and *A Lear of the Steppes* out of the library. I imagine myself as the young Russian in *Torrents of Spring* who wanders around a German town and meets a young girl serving in a tea shop with whom he falls in love and fights a duel. I should like to go to Germany.

September 5. MRS WOOLF COMPOSES

The Woolfs have returned from Rodmell. Mrs W came
into the printing room to set up type. We are printing a
new volume of poems by a man called Herbert Palmer.*
She was in a very gay mood and said she had been on the
loose in London. I somehow felt a bit disapproving, perhaps because I am guilty about my own wanderings when
I should be at the Press. She reads the most extraordinary
books, such as *The Sexual Life of Savages.* She left later
with L W and called out to Ma Cartwright for an address.
When she was told it was 25, Laburnum Grove, she
retailed it to L W as 'The Laurels, Winchester Avenue'
and had to be corrected by Ma Cartwright. L W gave a
cry of anguish. He is the magician who keeps us all going
by his strength of will – like the one in the *Tales of Hoffmann* – and Mrs W is a beautiful magical doll, very precious, but sometimes rather uncontrollable. Perhaps, like
the doll, she hasn't got a soul. But when she feels inclined,
she can create fantasy and we all fall over ourselves, or are
disapproving.

September 10. RIVALRY AND A BLOOMSBURY
EVENING

Today I learnt that Miss Belcher has secretly done a
design for the cover of *Dawn on Mont Blanc* and has shown
it to L W. My own typographical design of thick and thin

*Herbert Edward Palmer (1879–1961). Poet and critic. From 1899 was a
master in various English, French and German schools, but gave up teaching
in 1921. *The Judgement of François Villon,* 1927 and *The Dragon of Tingalam,*
1945, are plays. His *Collected Poems* appeared in 1932 and in that year he was
awarded a Civil List pension for distinction as a poet.

rules on pink paper can be printed on the machine and I pointed out to LW how expensive it would be to use Miss Belcher's, which is a realistic drawing and a surprisingly good one. He agreed, rather reluctantly. He seemed to find my agitation rather amusing. But if Miss Belcher can beat me at designing when she can do everything else so much better than I, I haven't much chance of LW keeping me on after my holiday.

However, the day ended very well, as he invited me round for the evening to meet the American publisher, Mr Harcourt, who has bought C. H. B. Kitchen's book, *Death of My Aunt*, and wants to use my cover design on the American edition.

I sat next to Mrs W who rolled her shag cigarettes on a tray in front of her. I think I must be practically the only person who can smoke them. We drank wine and talked about Lawrence. I thought they meant T E, but actually it was another Lawrence of whom I had never heard. They discussed what he ought to do in order to make some money. Apparently he suffers from T B. Mrs W held the stage and talked about working-class writers being under a disadvantage, like women, as writers. Roger Fry thought it was easier to be a painter than a writer if you were working class, as a painter did not have to have an ear for subtle social distinctions as a writer did. Desmond MacCarthy talked about Gissing. Altogether it was a very uplifting evening and the American publisher, Mr Harcourt, treated me as if I were just as important as any of the others!

September 13. PORNOGRAPHY

LW sent me with a letter to a gallery which the police have closed down and I saw some of D. H. Lawrence's paintings. They all seemed to be pictures of himself in the nude, and were done pretty crudely. It looked as if he had taken off his clothes and then sat down and painted himself: working in the nude at the nude. They made me think of a coal miner after his bath.

The Woolfs are taking his part over the prosecution.

INTELLECTUAL COMPANIONSHIP

LW and I have had long discussions about pornography on our walks round the Square. It seems he condones it when it's to do with sex, but doesn't enjoy lavatory humour — eschatology I think the word is. I agree with his point of view. In his *Ceylon Short Stories* he seems to imply that supreme sexual satisfaction with a beautiful girl ends in disillusion unless there is intellectual companionship. I wonder if he had a beautiful native girl as a mistress.

FILTH PACKETS AND DEATH PACKETS

I had better not press him too far about sex. Apparently the Bloomsbury crowd now talk about 'death packets' and 'filth packets'. 'Death packets' drag you down with morbid descriptions of their misfortunes, illnesses, etc. 'Filth packets' insist on wallowing in sexual matters. Actually, LW accused me of being a 'filth packet' this morning because my table was so untidy, so perhaps the term is pretty elastic.

First day back from my holiday in Germany. Tomorrow I go down to spend the week-end with the Woolfs at Rodmell. If LW had decided not to keep me on, I don't think he would have asked me down. I hope he doesn't ask me a lot of questions about Leipzig. I can't very well tell him I spent all my holiday standing about on a street corner and going to different dance halls trying to find a girl whose address I had lost, called Ilse.

Have given up attempting to read General Marbot's memoirs in French.

A WEEK-END AT RODMELL

Arrived in time for tea. The Woolfs were listening to a talk by Sir Oliver Lodge on the radio. It interested me, but they were very contemptuous of him and his belief in a spiritual world. Desmond MacCarthy came in. He had been out for a walk with Pinker. He talked about dogs, saying how bored they got. Apparently he works very hard, sitting up till two and three in the morning writing his articles for the *Sunday Times*. He has a son who is a medical student and a daughter who is very pretty and who is trying to get on the stage. Not quite the thing for a member of Bloomsbury to do.

LW and I walked in the garden while Mrs W got the supper ready. He gave me a book on double-entry book-keeping and another one on publishing by Unwin, which he said was very sound. He believes that anyone can do anything they really want to – that I can master accounts. He says accounts are beautiful and waste is ugly. He showed me his compost heap with pride.

After supper we sat by the fire. Mrs W sat some way back by the lamp knitting – an occupation that was new to her.

I started talking about the Golden Section. This was silly as it roused the sleeping dogs in L W. I said there was some mathematical significance in the proportions of the Golden Section which could be demonstrated by a quadratic equation. Thus an argument followed on how to do quadratic equations during which L W shouted 'Liar!' 'Absurd!' 'Why!' until Mrs W had to pour oil on troubled waters by reminding him that 'Richard is a guest.' He always calls me 'Kennedy'.

I got up early as LW had asked me if I liked rising early and I had assured him I did. The house was quite silent. There was rather a bad smell about, which I assumed came from the cesspool. It was a lovely sunny morning and I walked across the water meadows to a beautiful stream.

When I got back LW was up smoking his pipe and seemed pleased to see me. He told me that we were going over to see the Bells at Charleston for the day. So after breakfast I went with him in his Singer to Lewes to do some shopping. Children pounded along the village pavement. 'The first day of school' remarked LW, his features softening. I thought of the winter term and standing behind the scrum on a sticky day, waiting for someone to make a break for the line.

We all went for a long walk over the Downs and then had a picnic. Vanessa Bell fell down a bank on her bottom and I guffawed with laughter, although no one else even smiled. Somewhere in the distance came the wail of a child. 'Stung!' cried Mrs W pouring coffee out of a Thermos flask. After lunch we all straggled home over the Downs. LW stopped to have a pee in a very casual sort of way without attempting to have any sort of cover. I could see this was a part of his super-rational way of living. Clive Bell boasted that he was unable to make a cup of tea – which aroused my contempt. He is the member of the Bloomsbury Set I like the least. Uncle George tells me that Boris Anrep has depicted Clive Bell and Diana Guinness in his mosaic on the floor of the National Gallery. I can well believe this after reading Clive Bell's *Civilization*, which describes people doing nothing but enjoy themselves while others work to support them. He is the opposite to LW.

Quentin Bell, a red-headed young man, told me quite

casually that he was taking up painting. No urge on his part to get behind the counter.

LW and Mrs W drove me to the station to catch my train. Mrs W's little niece came in the car with us and she and Mrs W sat in the back. Mrs W kept up a flow of absolutely absurd conversation with the child in a high pitched voice, using a crazy language made up of unrecognizable sounds.

At Lewes we had tea in a rather dreary teashop. I said that I thought Julian Bell's long hair looked sloppy and Mrs W said rather tartly that getting one's hair cut was a terrible bore. Following the path of reason seems to involve having no truck with convention. I wish now I had not given myself away.

THE FIRST YEAR ENDS

The leaves are starting to pile up in the Square. Pinker scurries about in them. Maynard Keynes and Lopokova are being blown along – a vast ship accompanied by a trim little tug.

L W showed me how to light my pipe facing the wind.

The lights go on early in the office. There is much talk of Mrs W's new book, *Orlando*, and plenty of tension.

L W came down with one of the new copies of *Orlando* just back from the binders. It's got a picture of Victoria Sackville-West on the cover. I managed to get hold of it in my lunch hour. It is supposed to be a biography of Mrs Nicolson: she begins as a boy in Elizabethan times and changes into a woman while living through the centuries. I think I'm going to like it much more than *To the Lighthouse*, which is a good thing because it's embarrassing to like someone and not admire their work.

A BEST SELLER

All hands to the pumps with *Orlando*. Mrs W, Ma Cartwright, Miss Belcher and I all lined up at the packing bench and slashed away with our butchers knives in order to send out review copies of *Orlando*. I took them to the Post Office in relays. Mrs W is a pretty fast worker considering she's not a professional like Miss Belcher and myself.

Orlando is selling like hot cakes. L W is terrified we will run out of stock and it's my job to keep count of the packages that have come from the binders. I count them several times a day, but there are always fewer than I expect.

Several people have called to congratulate Mrs W: Desmond MacCarthy and the Nicolsons and old Herbert Palmer, but he only wanted a copy of his *Villon*. His nose looks very blue. Miss B gave him a cup of tea.

Mrs W has bought a very smart winter outfit: long Russian-style black Cossack coat with astrakhan Russian hat – all much admired by Miss B.

Gordon & Gotch Export came round after the office was closed. Miss B and Ma Cartwright had left and I was working in the print room. He hammered on the door and demanded 200 copies of *Orlando*. That left only eight packages.

LW was out. I shall have to tell him first thing on Monday and he'll certainly have kittens, as there's bound to be a big run at the beginning of the week after our advertisement in the *Observer*.

As I was leaving, a large rat ran across the floor of the office towards Mrs W's studio. Ma Cartwright will be horrified when I tell her.

Still very cold and a hard frost. Ma Cartwright arrived very late carrying a lot of shopping in her arms. She had some difficulty descending the area steps.

LW was in great spirits and asked me if I could get

hold of some skates and suggested going skating in Richmond Park. I took this to mean that I had the morning off. Despite black looks from Ma Cartwright and Miss Belcher I went out in search of skates and eventually obtained some at a greengrocers in Marchmont Street, very inefficient wooden ones that strapped on to one's feet.

After lunch we set out for Richmond in the Singer. Pinker had to come with us which proved to be a mistake. LW had some skates with curly ends. I asked him if they were racing skates. He said he didn't know, but he had had them since he was a boy.

Practically the whole of London was on the ice. I met my cousin, who is a medical student, showing off to a dark-haired girl in a white sweater. There was a stall selling oranges and other stalls selling hot pies. It was just like the wonderful scene in *Orlando* when the Thames is frozen over.

Of course Pinker rushed after LW barking and went slithering about all over the ice. In the end we had to take it in turns to guard Pinker while the others skated.

When the sun started to sink we climbed back into the car, lighted our pipes and drove to LW's brother's house in East Sheen.

MRS ANREP GIVES A PARTY

When I told LW that I was going to Mrs Anrep's party, he said, 'I suppose she's taking advantage of Roger Fry being in Manchester.'

I asked him if I should wear my dinner jacket (which I had only just got – it belonged to my uncle). He said he did not think so.

I was a bit embarrassed when Mrs Anrep pressed me to say what I thought about Mrs W's books. I know I was expected, as the new young man at the Hogarth Press, to say something brilliant for the benefit of the group that had collected round us. The truth was that I had only really read *Orlando*, *Mrs Dalloway* and *The Common Reader*. The other books I had found rather heavy going and had skimmed through.

I said I didn't think she created characters as well as a writer like Turgenev. I could see this didn't go down at all well and felt rather like Peter denying Christ.

I met a chap called Birrell who said he had also worked for the Hogarth Press and was I a 'factotum'. I said I supposed I was. 'More totem than fact, I should imagine,' he said.

He asked me if L W still made the staff use proofs in the wc. I said 'Good Lord, no!' But as a matter of fact, Miss B has had an awful job getting him to let the office join the clean towel service.

Rachel MacCarthy was there. She is the most beautiful girl with a smooth glossy head like a seagull. She was wearing a dark green frock with small flowers on it that came up to the neck, and black stockings.

As usual she was surrounded by a crowd of young men. Someone said she was a frightfully stupid girl and would never get anywhere with her acting. This made me feel extremely sympathetic towards her, though I felt the remark was prompted by sour grapes. She seemed to me a lot more intelligent than the other girls there.

There was another young man there called Raymond Mortimer about whom everyone was talking. Apart from being a contributor to *The Nation*, he was doing a terrific line with Sylva Norman* who is one of our authors.

Mrs W wrote a blurb for her novel about Spain. It looks so easy when she does it – she just jotted it down on a piece of typing paper: 'Miss Norman's novel is a delightful mixture of fact and fantasy' etc. I had spent hours trying to make something out of what was on the leaflet.

I talked to Tomlin, a sculptor, about an exhibition of

*Sylva Norman (b. Manchester 1901). The Hogarth Press published her book *Nature has no Tune*.

drawings by Gaudier Brzeska I had seen at Bumpus. I have been practising this type of drawing and am going to the zoo on Saturday to do some.

Someone brought Count Potocki,* who was wearing his red cassock. He caused quite a stir. Somehow I don't think he was invited.

I have seen him before – only the other day, near Victoria. He looks such a strange figure, striding along the foggy streets, like a ghost from the Middle Ages.

LETTER TO TODD

Dear Todd,

I am sorry we didn't see more of each other during the hols. I enjoyed the Alice White film.† As a matter of fact, I've been having rather a good time and am learning a lot. I know I described this place as the Revised Inferno and offered to show you round, whetting your appetite with some preliminary sketches. Unfortunately, your reply fell into the hands of LW who objects to Ma Cartwright and himself being referred to as Satan and Svengali.

I met a rather smart girl called Diana Mathias who asked me to dinner at her home which turned out to be a vast mansion in the middle of Mayfair. I should have worn my dinner jacket.

Unfortunately, I forgot to bring a handkerchief and she sent the footman for one of her father's which he brought to me on a silver salver.

We went to the flicks. She stood up very correctly for God Save the King *while I was searching for my new black hat*

---

*Count Potocki claimed to be the rightful King of Poland. He was aided by LW in his defence against publishing obscene poetry.
†Alice White starred in *Show of Shows*, Warner Brothers (1929).

with a very broad brim that was getting trampled to death under the feet of less patriotic people.

The next evening I went to a song recital at her house. This time I did wear my dinner jacket, and also an opera hat — the kind that flips in and out. Unfortunately, no one actually saw me wearing it except the footman to whom I handed it.

I got a lift home from a very wild looking girl with a shock
of fair hair and two other people in a Bugatti, so I did not put
my hat on in case it blew off. I was sitting perched up at the
back, hanging on for dear life. We went to a roadhouse which
had a swimming bath. The fair haired girl tried to bathe naked
and we all got thrown out. Altogether my opera hat was rather
an embarrassment to me, especially when I said goodbye to the
girl and it suddenly flipped out.

Almost everyone in London was at the party. Robert Lynd of the News Chronicle *told me to 'cast my bread upon the waters'. Ernest Milton had just finished playing Othello. I asked him if the bed had made him sleepy.*

I asked a chap for a light and when he gave me one I forgot to thank him. 'Why the bloody hell can't you say thank you!' he exclaimed. I was glad to see that Rachel MacCarthy was some distance away out of earshot. She had her usual throng of young men around her. I was going to join the group when I felt a shove in the back. I turned round to see Uncle George. 'What are you doing?' I exclaimed. 'Pushing you in the right direction,' he replied.

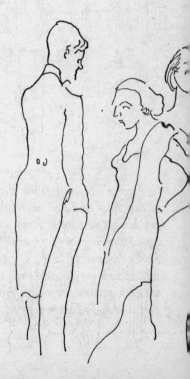

Diana Mathias evidently thinks I'm a farouche literary
young man with plenty of talent for drawing and writing. But
she tells me she has a French count who is 'very keen' on her.

I must finish now. Give my regards to Ma Webb. Is she
still giving you eggs for tea? I'm glad Kemble got his scholar-
ship. One in the eye for Bowie. Don't forget to mark your letter
PERSONAL *when you next write.*

Yours,
Drowse

ON THE ROAD WITH ORLANDO – FIRST DAY

The success of *Orlando* has persuaded LW that it might
be worthwhile sending me out into the wilderness – in
other words, the provinces, to sell the Press's books. Unfortunately, I have got too many of them in my suitcase.
'How that case weighs me down.' He made me write to
make appointments with all the booksellers and plan an
itinerary.

This is the first day of it and am writing this in the
smoking room of the Royal Hotel, Manchester, having
travelled down from Nottingham where I succeeded in
selling only two copies of *Orlando*. These were to a poor
old bookseller in the market who said he suffered from
his heart and couldn't smoke his pipe. What a terrible
thing it must be to be old and not be able to smoke your
pipe.

I have interrupted my reading of *The Revolt of the
Angels* by Anatole France to write this. I think it is the
funniest book I have ever read. I burst into laughter and
couldn't control myself for some time. Everyone in the
smoking room turned round to stare at me. Now they
have gone back to listening to the wireless.

Travelled to Edinburgh by the night train after spending half the day in Manchester and half in Liverpool. Sales very bad.

There was a man in the carriage on the train to Edinburgh with a beautiful Clumber spaniel.

I plan to take the afternoon off and go to the roller skating rink and then the Dunedin Palais de Dance.

ON THE ROAD — THIRD DAY

Last night I went to the Dunedin Palais de Dance as well as roller skating. The Scottish skaters are pretty tough, if they knock you down they don't trouble to help you up.

At the Palais de Dance I stood for a long time not able to make up my mind which girl to ask for a dance until almost the last one. Then I asked a girl in a blue dress with fair hair.

We walked on to the floor together. Her waist had a lot of give in it.

She soon cottoned on to the fact that I didn't know the steps and managed to steer me about so expertly that I seemed to be doing quite well. When the music stopped I took her arm, but she unhooked it and took mine. I asked her if she would like to have a cup of coffee and she said she would if her friend could come too.

It was raining when we emerged. There an old woman holding on to the railings opposite. We stood in the entrance watching her as the rain pelted down. Her hands slid slowly down the railings until finally she rolled on to the pavement and into the gutter. The water pouring down the hill streamed over her. I was going to her assistance, but the two girls stopped me.

I spent the morning in Edinburgh and travelled to Glasgow this afternoon. Sold only two sets of *Hogarth Lectures on Literature*. These are practically the only books you can sell here and, of course, *Orlando*: twenty-five copies of *Orlando* to Menzies.

In the Glasgow station buffet there is a strange-looking girl – almost a dwarf – selling tea. She looks like a water fairy from a mysterious and cavernous Scottish loch. Incongruously seated behind tea urns and a cash register, she is a minute figure wrapped in a black shawl, with green eyes in a small triangular face and a mass of black greasy curls. The mirrors and glass bottles give the impression of a subterranean cave. She says the same thing to every customer, 'Sugar and milk in your tea?' If I come back in a year's time, she will still be saying it.

Still pouring with rain. I returned to Edinburgh late yesterday after a very disappointing day.

The buyers are very friendly and ready to discuss Gerald Gould's articles in the *Observer*, but they won't really buy. They don't like our covers and say the public don't like them. LW ought to let me do more. Went to the Palais again, but the girl I had met on the previous day was not there, neither was her friend, although they had promised to meet me. Had some whisky. The Scots seem to drink nothing else.

Got up early today and caught a train to Sheffield — still raining when I arrived in this gloomy town. I had only sold £20 worth of books on the whole tour when I arrived here today. I felt very depressed. I decided to try the public library to see what I could do there. The Librarian was very agreeable and gave me a cup of tea. I showed him all the books in my case and one by one made suitable comments. When I came to *Stavrogin's Confession — A supposed chapter in the life of a great sinner* by Dostoyevsky I felt I should tell him that I didn't think his readers would be interested in the book.

'So you think we are completely uncivilized up here, do you?' he exclaimed. 'I'll have ten copies!'

Altogether he has given an order for £100 worth of books.

I went to the flicks in the evening.

In my hotel bedroom there is a notice saying 'This hotel is run by, with and for men on the road'. Well, this man on the road has saved his bacon. I look forward to confronting LW with some proof of my magic touch as a salesman.

Another Christmas has passed at the Hogarth Press. Trees in the Square all bare and black. LW tells me Mrs W is ill – just over-tired after holiday in Germany.

AN ACCIDENT WITH A SHELF

A very cold day. I suppose it was bound to happen some time, but my shelf has fallen down and I shall never have the heart to put it up again.

Lord Oliver came into the Press muffled to the eyes in an enormous overcoat from which the top of his bald pate emerged. The original member of the Cranium Club I should think.

For some reason LW came down to talk to him in the office. They sat down facing us in two chairs and launched into a very profound conversation about Africa, during which I was aware of a series of creaks and then a sudden crack and, looking up, saw my shelf suddenly dip down at the corner. One or two leaflets floated gracefully down and alighted at the feet of the two men. But they continued their conversation. Another crack, the shelf dipped ominously again and more leaflets glided down, covering the carpet. But the two men continued unconcernedly puffing their pipes.

A snigger from Miss B caused me to look at her sternly. She seemed to be bent double and had her hand over her mouth. I thought this showed very bad breeding.

Then, like a ship sinking, the shelf slowly started to

subside, leaflets pouring off and floating down like snow flakes.

I watched helplessly as they cascaded onto LW and Lord Oliver, burying them almost to their knees. They calmly rose, as if nothing had occurred, shook themselves and silently went upstairs.

Miss B was lying prostrate over her typewriter choking.

THREE POETS

Three young men put their heads round our basement door and looked at us as if we were the seven dwarfs. They were all wearing brightly coloured scarves. They had brought with them a volume of poetry on which they had collaborated. They had all just come from Cambridge.

When LW appeared they showed suitable signs of respect.

I saw Roger Fry in the bank this morning when I took in the cheques. He was wearing a heavily patched trench coat which came down to his ankles. His long grey hair stuck out in a fringe between the brim of his hat and his collar.

A young man came into the Press. He was wearing an open-neck shirt and a velvet jacket and had a charming smile. He told me he had been doing drawings of a near-by church that was being pulled down. I had some difficulty in adjusting to this informal approach. It turned out that he was Duncan Grant and had called to see Virginia.

Uncle George surprised me when I asked him if he liked Clive Bell by saying he smelt a bit.

PROUST

In the printing room when Mrs W is setting type and I am machining we work in silence, unless, of course, she is in one of her happy moods – if she's going to a party or been walking round London, which she often does.

Today I interrupted her to ask her what Proust was like, as a reviewer had called her the 'English Proust'. At first she did not understand because I had pronounced Proust to rhyme with Faust and not boost. But she laughed and said she couldn't do French cooking, but it was very delicious.

LW'S GENEROSITY

Harold Nicolson and Victoria Sackville-West came into the Press. She was wearing her wide-brimmed cavalier hat and a black cape and he had on a very smart blue shirt.

Mr Palme Dutt came in to inquire about his book on Tagore and gave me a 2s. tip which amused Miss B. She said I could give it to her if I liked. Ma Cartwright was very obsequious to the Nicolsons.

She told us that LW was really very kind-hearted if you were in trouble, and could not help his fads. He had sent £100 to the Welsh miner poet Human Eye* because he was starving.

READER'S REPORT

MSS keep pouring into the Press, but it's a case of many are called and few are chosen. I've glanced at a few and would like to write a reader's report. I have thought of sending in an anonymous manuscript by myself. I wrote a story of an air woman on a flight to Australia and an old newspaper seller who is dying of an incurable disease. I read it to Uncle George, but he thought it too like *Mrs Dalloway*.

Miss B takes no interest in the books, but stumps out to lunch with a woman's magazine. I think she has read *Orlando*, but that's because Mrs Woolf gave her a signed copy. When I told her the right way to pronounce 'Proust', she made a face at me.

PROUST

LW is rather like Swann. I can easily imagine him threading his tie through a valuable ring instead of tying it in the usual way. I wish I dared do this. Proust probably wore suits made out of the same expensive-looking material as LW and a large black hat. No, probably he wore a top hat. Of course, Mrs W is not at all like Odette,

*Miss Belcher's name for Huw Menai.

81

but they are both rather wayward creatures, worshipped
by their husbands.

READER'S REPORT – CONTINUED

LW has given me two MSS to read and write reports on.
One is called *Sligo* by Jack Yeats and the other *Brothers
and Sisters* by Ivy Compton-Burnett.

Slig is very meandering with no story, but it is very
poetic. *Brothers and Sisters* has no atmosphere at all. I think
I will ask Uncle George's opinion of it as I would like to
say something intelligent.

I have got *Brothers and Sisters* back from Uncle George. He handed it to me and said, 'It's a work of genius. I can't say more.' This is rather exciting. I made out a very professional reader's report on a sheet of foolscap. I wrote a few lines about *Sligo*, saying I did not think it had enough general appeal, although it had poetic qualities and plenty of atmosphere. Against *Brothers and Sisters* I just put A WORK OF GENIUS.

LW took my report and glanced at it. His lip curled when he read the words, but he did not say anything.

Perhaps I have discovered a genius and he will be eternally grateful to me.

LW gave me back the two MSS and told me to return them to their authors with the usual letter of rejection.

Evidently he doesn't think *Brothers and Sisters* 'a work of genius'.

'She can't even write,' he said, handing the manuscript to me. 'At least this man Yeats knows how to write.'

I managed to get Miss B to type the rejection letters in exchange for promising to take all the post.

LW is very keen to publish a book called *Undying Faces*,* a collection of photographs of Death Masks of famous men. This would be the second book we have done about death.

A DISAPPOINTED AUTHOR

Edwin Muir† came into the Press. For some reason I asked him for his card. He said he did not have a card.

Undying Faces, published in 1929.

†Edwin Muir. b. Orkneys 1887, d. 1959. Nordist poet and critic. Numerous books including *Life of John Knox*, 1929; *The Story and the Fable*, 1940 (an autobiography); and *The Structure of the Novel*, 1958.

I have become so used to Palme Dutt and his magnificent gestures that Edwin Muir seems a very modest man in comparison. He wears a beret. LW is very annoyed because, despite the fact that we first published his work, he is giving his next book to Cape who will give him better terms.

DISILLUSION

Since my shelf fell down I have been feeling very disillusioned and things have not seemed to be going so well. I would very much like to go to an art school.

I spoke to my Uncle George about it and he said, 'Let's see what you can do' and put a sort of alabaster Egyptian object, of which he thinks very highly, in front of me and told me to draw it. When I had finished he looked at it and said, 'You obviously have no idea of form.' This was rather discouraging.

LW and Uncle George are very opposite characters. When you ask LW a question he looks down at his toes. When you ask Uncle George something he looks up at the ceiling.

A PICNIC

I went with the Kennedys for a picnic in Richmond Park. We were accompanied by Brian Guinness and his beautiful wife, Diana, who reclined rather in the same pose as Boris Anrep gives her in his mosaic in the National Gallery.

She was wearing a calf-skin coat and Uncle George refused to eat anything until she had taken it off because he disapproves of this sort of thing.

We sang madrigals after consuming champagne and lobster sandwiches.

The trees in the Square are beginning to turn.

THE UNIFORM EDITION

L W is bringing out a uniform edition of Mrs W's books. He said I could try out some ideas for a typographical cover.

Miss B was sarcastic because I took Freud's *Collected Papers* to lunch with me. 'I suppose we shan't see him for the rest of the afternoon,' she said to Ma C.

I have invented a sort of tumbril with roller skate wheels to take the post to the Post Office. Everyone looks rather askance at it, but L W has made no comment. It saves Miss B and myself endless journeys with parcels of books, and we can get away much earlier.

PETTY CASH

A bad day today. L W came into the office and helped himself to some of the petty cash. Then, as always, he very deliberately took out his Onoto fountain pen and with a trembling hand entered the sum in the little red cash book.

He asked Miss B what 6d. 'toilet requisites' was for and she blushed. Ma C said rather crossly, 'Toilet paper, Mr Woolf.'

He finished adding up the petty cash book and checked it with the money in the little metal money box. Suddenly he gave a cry of vexation and tore out the pages of the book and threw them at me, shouting 'This is totally inaccurate!'

My writing has become so like his that Ma C and Miss

B can't tell the difference, especially as I've managed to introduce a wobble into it. This has led to some pretty acrimonious disputes in the office with Ma C accusing L W of making false entries in the ledgers, when the slip-up has been made by me. These mistakes usually happen on a Saturday morning when I am alone in the office. I find it easy to make mistakes when the telephone is ringing and Gordon & Gotch are demanding a selection of books that have to be searched for.

The system employed is that when a book is sold the money is entered in the petty cash book and then the cash ledger. An entry is made against the book in a third ledger which has five columns: the date, the name of the purchaser, number of copies sold, total number of copies of the book sold, including the sale just recorded and the amount of money taken.

AN EMBARRASSING INCIDENT

Evidently Miss B and I can't be left alone in the office together while Ma C is on holiday and Mrs W at Rodmell. This idea may have grown up because of an incident that happened the other day.

Miss B and I had gone into the studio while Mrs W was out to get some more copies of *Homage to Cézanne* as we couldn't fulfil an order without opening a bale. What we thought was the right bale turned out to be *Seducers in Ecuador*, so we had to pack that up again and heave another bale off its pile and open it. By the time we had done this and got it back into place we were breathing very heavily. Suddenly Ma C burst into the studio with her customary ferocity and glared at us. I don't know what she imagined.

It is very hot. Miss B and I spent the afternoon putting circulars into envelopes and watching the hands of the alarm clock. I caused the stamp machine, which Miss B has made L W purchase, to chew up a lot of stamps. It is sweltering in the basement and I should think all the drains of the Russell Hotel go under it, it's so whiffy in the back quarters.

Mrs W is working on another book. There is no printing to do. I went out and collected Ma C's daughters from Victoria where they were arriving from school and brought them back to the Press. They sat and watched

their mother and Miss B work. LW put his head in and was quite agreeable and they patted Pinker. But later he was sarcastic about Ma C's anxiety over her daughters, asking if she thought they were liable to be raped at any minute. He disapproves of my fetching them in firm's time.

Pinker seems mildly surprised to get attention from strangers. The other day when LW was making an entry in a ledger Pinker calmly climbed on a chair and licked his nose. They have got to look rather alike. Pinker's nose is getting rather grey. I suppose the time I have been here, two years, is rather a long time in a dog's life.

What am I talking about a dog's life for? The other day I was walking up the hill by Lord's cricket ground when I met a fellow going the same way. He told me he was going for an interview for a job. He said if he didn't get it he would commit suicide. He had been out of work for five years. I wished him luck.

A BLOOMSBURY CRICKET MATCH

We travelled down together. I don't think Uncle George was very keen. He may even have accepted the invitation because of me. He's a great believer in meeting people, but he hasn't got the manner of a social lion. He was reading *Rich Relatives* by Compton Mackenzie, an author practically on the Bloomsbury Index. I produced my volume of *A la Recherche du Temps Perdu*.

Uncle George gets his clothes made by some frightful tailor who lives in the wilds of Donegal and makes working men's Sunday suits. This is because he lets Aunt Mary buy them for him. He was wearing white trousers, a jacket and collar and tie – quite wrong for cricket. I was wearing my OM blazer. No one would think from looking

at him that Uncle George was an Old Etonian and won the poetry prize. He was feeling rather ill and complained of a pain in his back.

David Garnett gave us a very agreeable welcome and fed us beer and sandwiches. We went to the pavilion where Clive Bell was holding forth to a large audience about cricket being like a ballet. Uncle George seemed to spend most of his time explaining to people that he wasn't going to play because he had a slight chill. He seemed fairly popular, but would insist on sitting on the steps of the pavilion reading his Compton Mackenzie.

I was put to field long stop or fine point, whichever you like to make it. Desmond MacCarthy wasn't a very good wicket keeper so it was mostly long stop. James Strachey, who is very tall, was fielding point. He had very tight drainers on, but managed to get down to square cuts quite efficiently. I had some conversation with him. He seemed a philosophical type, ready to make the best of things such as when he was nearly hit on the head by a wide.

Clive Bell approached the crease rather like Serge Lifar. The umpire put him off by asking if he wanted to take guard. He made a ridiculous sort of cow shot the first ball, was lucky to connect and scored a boundary. The next ball went past Desmond MacCarthy full toss. He made a despairing gesture as the ball went past me. Everyone shouted 'Run'. By the time I had chased the ball and retrieved it, Clive Bell and the other batsman who happened to be Uncle George were both at the same end of the pitch arguing with each other.

I should say that Uncle George had been prevailed upon to go in to bat for his side, though he insisted that his lumbago made fielding out of the question.

Finally the ball was relayed back to the bowler who succeeded in stumping Clive Bell. He started to argue with the umpire in the most unsportsmanlike manner, making all sorts of allusions to Japanese literature. Absolutely not done!

Although Uncle George made twelve not out, it was a very lucky innings full of snicks and he was twice dropped. I had very bad luck in getting bowled first ball. I can't say that Uncle George and I had distinguished ourselves. His lumbago seemed to desert him on the journey home. and the Compton Mackenzie volume became decorated on its fly leaf and endpapers with numerous designs for windows and doors.

THE UNIFORM EDITION

LW is very taken up with the project of a Uniform Edition of Mrs Woolf's books. He came down and talked to Miss Ritchie about it. She is a very nice young woman who does the travelling for the London booksellers. She had dropped in for a cup of tea with us and to give in her orders.

Apparently it is all a great gamble.

LW explained to me that he proposed to have stereos made of the type in all Mrs W's books and to print from this and so avoid the cost of resetting. But as two of them have been printed for publishers other than ourselves, it is necessary to find a page size which is a common denominator for the different sizes of page that will give an adequate margin and not be too expensive.

This is just the sort of problem which he enjoys, but which defeats me.

A RIVAL FROM AN UNSUSPECTED QUARTER

Mr Gossling came in to talk to LW about the paper for the Uniform Edition. LW had a long confab with him in which Mr Gossling, after a lot of objections and talk about price, finally gave in.

Miss Ritchie came in with her beautiful sister who is at the Slade. She is doing a jacket for us. We had a discussion about how it could be printed. It looks as if she will be doing quite a few jackets for us which is very disheartening for me. Also, Vanessa Bell has done a very stylish typographical design for the Uniform Edition. I don't personally like her work, but I must admit it has style.

A PASSIONATE PILGRIM AND A UNIFORM EDITION

Final instructions from LW for the week I am to be on my own in the office. Apparently all problems connected with the Uniform Edition have been settled. My task will be simply to deal with the bagmen and cope with the orders coming in, which shouldn't be heavy in August.

I switched him onto 'Passionate Pilgrims' whom he mentions in his 'World of Books' article in the *New Statesman*. These are people dedicated to a single idea in life – like himself. I think in his case it's the Uniform Edition.

ON MY OWN

I am getting on better than I thought I would. LW and Mrs W have gone to Rodmell, Ma C has gone to her sister in Deal, and Miss B to Broadstairs. It's fun and gives me quite a sensation of power, being the sole representative of the Press.

Went to the pub for lunch. Gordon & Gotch Export was quite polite. The bagmen are taking me more seriously and there's a little less of the cockney humour.

I have moved into a room of my own so I am alone all day, but it's rather pleasant. I wish there was someone I could ring up.

Behind the house is what must be a hospital for barrel organs and you can look down into a yard from the landing window and see a whole mass of them and hear them. It's a sweet melancholy sound. On these hot evenings the yard is full of children who dance to the music. The street is very narrow and I can talk to some of the women patients in their ward at the Italian hospital, those who are up and in their dressing-gowns. One tall, dark one invited me over, so I went with some cakes from the café, but the Sister chased me out.

My room costs 12s. 6d. a week, bed & breakfast.

As I was going home after work yesterday, a girl said 'hallo' as I was passing the Russell Hotel. She was wearing a blue suit and looked rather pretty. I thought I must have met her at Mrs Anrep's. But as soon as she stated talking it was obvious she hadn't got the 'Bloomsbury voice'. It was too late to walk away, so I invited her to my digs. Unfortunately, as we were climbing the stairs we met the young man, Potter, who lives above me and he gave me a very black look. Once inside my room the girl drew the curtains and slipped off her skirt. She was wearing blue knickers like a schoolgirl's. When her blouse came off, I was horrified to see that the whole of the top of her body was most terribly sunburned. This so distressed me that I sat down on the bed. My heart had been thumping, but now I did not feel like making love. The girl said 'Never mind, darling. What about drawing me "nice" ?' indicating the drawings I had pinned up on the wall. But in the end I just made some tea and we talked. I did not do the drawings and she said she had to get back to work.

When we got outside a policeman stopped us and asked me if 'this woman' had accosted me, pointing at the girl. I replied that she was a friend I had met at a party. He looked very annoyed and for a moment I thought he was going to arrest me. The girl gave me a warm smile and slipped away.

When I got back to my digs I found Potter waiting for me holding a large bottle of disinfectant which he had been pouring down the lavatory. I got another lecture on the same lines as the policeman's.

Another very easy day at the Press. Mr Gossling came in and was very surprised to find me on my own. He said he had never seen anyone progress so fast in the pub-

lishing business. I showed him my cover for *Death of my Aunt* which undoubtedly impressed him. He told me he had just dropped in to iron out a few small difficulties about the paper size for the Uniform Edition and that I could do it just as well as LW. He added that LW had got his sums slightly wrong. I said Mr Woolf was never wrong. He replied that we all make mistakes some time.

We went to a pub for a sandwich and a drink and in the end I told him to do just what he thought best about the paper. After all, Spalding & Hodge make the stuff, and, as he says, he has been in paper since he was a boy so he should know.

As I was going home this evening I had a great surprise. I bought my *Evening Standard* from the newspaper seller who looks as if he is suffering from an incurable disease. I turned to the book page, which is written by Arnold Bennett, to see if he was reviewing any of our books. The first thing I saw was a headline: A WORK OF GENIUS after which was written 'Miss Ivy Compton-Burnett's new novel is a work of genius.' So Uncle George was right, after all. I wonder what LW will say. He should have taken my advice.

Had supper in the ABC and read Proust. All going very smoothly at the Press.

CATASTROPHE

LW has returned from Rodmell in a towering rage. Apparently the whole Uniform Edition project has been ruined by me because I have unwittingly instructed Spalding & Hodge to cut the paper the wrong size.

LW brought back a number of sacks of apples and potatoes from Rodmell and I tried to help him hump them up the stairs, but he would not accept any assistance from me. He refuses to speak to me. He had Gossling in and gave him a terrific tongue lashing. Gossling's cheeks went quite pale.

I suppose I have really got the sack. L W says I can't be trusted to do anything but wrap up parcels and that I am the most frightful idiot he has ever had the privilege of meeting in a long career of suffering fools.

CATASTROPHE CONT'D

Wrapped up parcels all day. LW is still irate and glares at me.

Mrs C tells me that LW and Mrs W have invited a new author to tea and if she comes to the Press she must be shown upstairs. I asked who the author was.

'It's a lady called Miss Burnett.'

'Not Ivy Compton-Burnett! I must tell LW at once.'

When he came down at lunchtime he didn't give me an opportunity to speak to him so I ran after him and caught him on the stairs going up to his flat. I tried to tell him that we had refused Ivy Compton-Burnett's first book, but he looked at me quite uncomprehendingly and ran his hand through his hair.

'Never mind now, Richard,' he said in quite a kindly voice.

Well, I suppose it doesn't really matter. I'm leaving at the end of the month.

CATASTROPHE AND SOLUTION

These last days are torture. No sympathy from Miss B. I was glad to get out of the office and take some books to Dr Flügel at University College. I was walking through the cloisters looking for his department when three girls came swinging towards me with their arms linked. Three pairs of breasts and three laughing faces. They looked so happy and carefree. I thought of that basement prison, and acting on the spur of the moment, I sought out the authorities and learnt that there was a course of journalism starting in the autumn. Mr Solomon, who was in charge of the course, told me that a School Certificate was a necessary qualification for taking the course, but in my case it could be waived owing to my experience with the Hogarth Press, which undoubtedly impressed him.

A small legacy from my grandmother enabled me to take the course.

How right LW was when he told me on one of our walks round the Square that a little capital was one of the most important things in life.

THE HOGARTH PRESS

[about 1928]

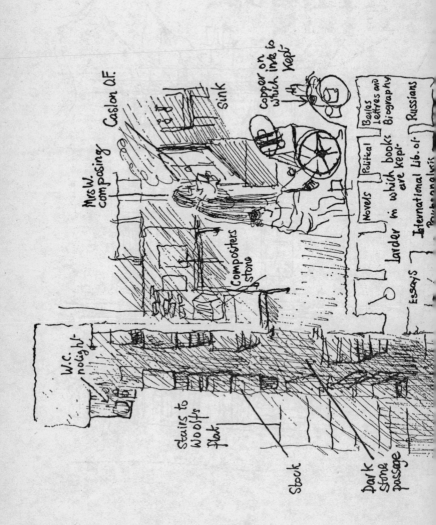

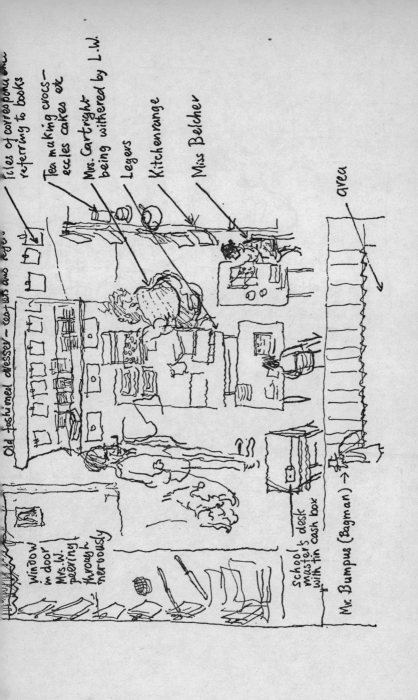

Old fashioned dresser — copies and keys

files of correspondence and — referring to books

Tea making cross — eccles cakes etc

Mrs. Cartright being withered by L.W.

Legers

Kitchen range

Miss Belcher

window in door Mrs.W. peering through nervously

School master's desk with tin cash box

Mr. Bumpus (Bagman) →

area

large windowless
room in which large bales of books
were kept and in which Mrs W. wrote
her books

MORE ABOUT PENGUINS
AND PELICANS

Penguinews, which appears every month, contains details of all the new books issued by Penguins as they are published. From time to time it is supplemented by our stocklist which is our list of almost 5,000 titles.

A specimen copy of *Penguinews* will be sent to you free on request. Please write to Dept EP, Penguin Books Ltd, Harmondsworth, Middlesex, for your copy.

In the U.S.A.: For a complete list of books available from Penguins in the United States write to Dept CS, Penguin Books, 625 Madison Avenue, New York, New York 10022.

In Canada: For a complete list of books available from Penguins in Canada write to Penguin Books Canada Ltd, 2801 John Street, Markham, Ontario L3R 1B4.

Recent autobiographies and memoirs in Penguins:

HERMIT OF PEKING
THE HIDDEN LIFE OF SIR EDMUND BACKHOUSE
Hugh Trevor-Roper

The memoirs of a distinguished Chinese scholar revealed a fantastically different person. Hugh Trevor-Roper uses these memoirs to tell the tale of one of the most outrageous forgers, confidence tricksters and eccentrics of the century.

THE ENCHANTED PLACES
Christopher Milne

With deftness and artistry, Milne draws a memorable portrait of his father and evokes the Hundred Acre Wood, Galleons Lap and the Poohsticks Bridge – the 'enchanted places' of his childhood in Sussex.

'Mr Milne has set out to re-create a world . . . he has been totally successful' – *The Times Literary Supplement*

SELECTED LETTERS
D. H. Lawrence

Never intended for publication, these letters reveal a compulsive autobiography of Lawrence; a personal record of his early life on the knife-edge of maturity, his later literary and personal friendships, and his wanderings, driven by the demons within him, through Europe and Mexico.

THE DEATH OF THE KING'S CANARY

Dylan Thomas and John Davenport

Hilary Byrd threw a wild party to celebrate his Poet Laureateship. Every shade of human eccentricity was there, from a fuddled old duke to a dope-smoking butler. There were polite dwarfs, mincing poofs, bloated poets, hungry nymphomaniacs, a vodka-sodden Nobel prizewinner; there were Harry Bartatt, the Yorkshire sculptor, and Eric Wetley, dressed entirely in rubber.

In this harshly witty dunciad, Dylan Thomas and John Davenport conspired to lampoon some of their most distinguished contemporaries. In 1941, these ruthless caricatures virtually amounted to scabrous libels – now when their impact is softened, we can delight in brutal parodies of T. S. Eliot, W. H. Auden, Stephen Spender, Augustus John, Henry Moore and many more – including the authors themselves.

And besides all this – who killed the 'King's Canary'?

'Brilliantly uncharitable' – *The Times* (London)

' . . . a splendid joke' – *Daily Telegraph*

'Glorious reading' – *Boston Globe*

D. H. Lawrence

THE RAINBOW

The Brangwens have been established for generations as a yeoman family on the borders of Nottinghamshire, among the coal-mines – a vigorous and strong-willed breed. When Tom marries a Polish widow, however, he finds that love must come to terms with the other forces in his personality.

WOMEN IN LOVE

This novel, which Lawrence considered his best, tells the lives and emotional conflicts of two sisters in a Midlands colliery town. Ursula falls in love with Birkin (a self-portrait of Lawrence) and Gudrun has a tragic affair with Gerald, the son of the local colliery owner. The four of them clash in passion, thought and belief and their deeply held convictions about love and modern society.

AARON'S ROD

Aaron is a respected member of the mining community, but it stifles him. Pinning his faith on his flute-playing, he breaks with his wife, moves south . . . and meets Rawdon Lilly. The extraordinary relationship between these two men is the central span of this important novel.

SONS AND LOVERS

The Morel family live on the Nottinghamshire coalfield. Mrs Morel is disillusioned with her coarse-grained and hard-drinking husband, and centres all her expectations on her sons, especially Paul. As Paul grows older, tensions develop in their relationship, and his passions for two other women create a fatal conflict of love and possessiveness.

Angus Wilson

A BIT OFF THE MAP
AND OTHER STORIES

It was the decade of rubber plants, Espresso bars and skiffle, of Seuz, Teddy boys and Angry Young Men. These eight short stories are brilliant and incisive reflections on the pre-occupations and secrets of the 'respectable' middle classes of the fifties.

ANGLO-SAXON ATTITUDES

The grotesque idol discovered in Bishop Eorpwald's tomb has scandalized, mystified and inspired a whole generation of scholars. Gerald Middleton, one of the members of the excavation, keeps a further, more disreputable secret . . .

Separated from his sentimental Danish wife, Gerald is acutely aware of the void at the centre of his existence. But the world is reaching out to reclaim him . . .

AS IF BY MAGIC

Hamo Langmuir flies westward round the world to examine the effects of his miraculous high-yielding rice, leaving a bleak and impotent existence behind him. His god-daughter travels with her magic of myths and mysticism along the hippy trail to the East. They meet in Goa.

'Enough thought, comedy, wit, excitement and pathos to keep a dozen less profligate and inventive novelists busy for years' – Francis King in the *Observer*

Iris Murdoch

THE SANDCASTLE

Once again Iris Murdoch demonstrates that her gift for compelling narrative, vivid characterization and comic invention are unrivalled. Her story – of a frustrated middle-aged and unhappily married schoolmaster who falls hopelessly in love with a bewitching young artist – succeeds brilliantly in involving our emotions at every level.

A FAIRLY HONOURABLE DEFEAT

Rupert and Hilda are perfectly matched; their only worries, a drop-out son and Morgan, Hilda's unstable sister just back from America.

Enter Julius, Morgan's ex-lover, determined to give their seemingly impregnable marriage a mild jolt.

He sets the stage and distributes roles amongst his unwitting cast with unnerving brilliance and high comedy . . . until the last act with its final (but not altogether disgraceful) defeat.

FORTHCOMING IN 1979:

THE ITALIAN GIRL

There seems to be no limit to the self-destructive cancer of this family divided against itself. Never has Miss Murdoch used to greater effect her unique talent for laying bare the deepest and most secret places of a human soul.

Graham Greene

BRIGHTON ROCK

Set in the pre-war underworld of Brighton, this is the story of Pinkie, a teenage gangster whose ambitions and hatreds are horribly fulfilled – until Ida determines to convict him of murder.

THE POWER AND THE GLORY

Too human for heroism, too humble for martyrdom, the little, worldly Mexican 'whisky priest' is impelled towards his squalid Calvary as much by his own compassion for humanity as by the efforts of his pursuers during an anti-clerical purge.

THE END OF THE AFFAIR

This frank, intense account of a love-affair tells of the strange and callous steps taken by a middle-aged writer to destroy, or perhaps to reclaim, the mistress who had unaccountably left him eighteen months before.

OUR MAN IN HAVANA

Agent 59200/5 Wormold invented the stories he sent to the British Secret Service from Cuba . . . and the results surprised him more than anyone.

Also published by Penguin:

A BURNT-OUT CASE
THE HEART OF THE MATTER
THE QUIET AMERICAN · LOSER TAKES ALL
IT'S A BATTLEFIELD · JOURNEY WITHOUT MAPS
THE COMEDIANS
TRAVELS WITH MY AUNT